WOMEN
GROUNDBREAKERS

WOMEN IN THE MILITARY

Miriam Coleman

PowerKiDS
press™

New York

Published in 2016 by The Rosen Publishing Group, Inc.
29 East 21st Street, New York, NY 10010

First Edition

Editor: Sarah Machajewski
Book Design: Reann Nye

Photo Credits: Cover (background) untitled/Shutterstock.com; cover (Hopper), p. 29 Cynthia Johnson/ The LIFE Images Collection; cover (Nightingale), p. 9 Hulton Archive/Getty Images; cover (Barton), p. 13 Buyenlarge/Archive Photos/Getty Images; p. 5 http://commons.wikimedia.org/wiki/File:Leigh_Ann_ Hester_medal.jpg; p. 7 DEA/M. SEEMULLER/De Agostini/Getty Images; p. 11 Everett Historical/ Shutterstock.com; p. 15 Apic/Hulton Archive/Getty Images; p. 17 MPI/Archive Photos/Getty Images; p. 19 Keystone/Hulton Archive/Getty Images; p. 21 U.S. Department of Agriculture/https://www.flickr.com/ photos/expertinfantry/5467551836/CC BY-ND 2.0; p. 23 (Wolfenbarger) Thos Robinson/ Getty Images Entertainment/Getty Images; p. 23 (Howard) Chip Somodevilla/Getty Images News/Getty Images; p. 23 (Dunwoody) Kris Connor/Getty Images Entertainment/Getty Images; p. 25 http://commons.wikimedia. org/wiki/File:Lt._Gen._Patricia_D._Horoho.jpg; p. 27 Alex Wong/Getty Images News/Getty Images.

Cataloging-in-Publication Data

Coleman, Miriam.
Women in the military / by Miriam Coleman.
p. cm. — (Women groundbreakers)
Includes index.
ISBN 978-1-4994-1052-5 (pbk.)
ISBN 978-1-4994-1088-4 (6 pack)
ISBN 978-1-4994-1100-3 (library binding)
1. United States — Armed Forces — Women — Juvenile literature. 2. Women soldiers — United States — Juvenile literature. I. Coleman, Miriam. II. Title.
UB418.W65 C65 2016
355'.0082'0973—d23

CONTENTS

WOMEN WARRIORS

Sergeant Leigh Ann Hester of the Kentucky National Guard was helping guide a supply **convoy** in Iraq in 2005. When the convoy was attacked by a group of **insurgents** armed with weapons, Hester bravely fought back, defeating the insurgents and leading her team to safety. She was the first woman to receive the Silver Star medal for close-quarters combat.

Women have been serving on battlefields around the world for thousands of years. In the United States, women have served in the armed forces since the Revolutionary War. Although their official roles were once limited to supporting soldiers as nurses, cooks, and messengers, groundbreaking women have steadily expanded their opportunities. Women now fly fighter planes, drive tanks, command **battalions**, and more.

AMAZING ACHIEVEMENTS

The Silver Star is the U.S. military's third-highest decoration of **valor**. Hester was the first woman to receive it since World War II, when a group of army nurses received the honor for evacuating a hospital that was under attack.

Brave women like Sergeant Leigh Ann Hester have helped create opportunities for women throughout all levels of the military.

DRIVEN BY FAITH

When Joan of Arc was about 13 years old, she believed she heard the voice of God telling her to go into battle. It was 1425, and France was under attack by the English in the Hundred Years' War. Joan couldn't read or write, yet she convinced the French prince Charles of Valois that God had given her a mission to drive out the English and make Charles king.

When Joan was 18, she led an army of several hundred men to victory against the English at Orléans in 1429. Her forces captured several towns for France, helping the French prince become King Charles VII. Joan continued leading attacks against the English and their allies, but she was captured in 1430. She was charged with witchcraft and **heresy**, and was burned alive.

Joan of Arc's story has inspired people for centuries. There are countless paintings, movies, and books about her remarkable life.

REVOLUTIONARY IN DISGUISE

When the American Revolution began in 1775, many colonists answered the call of duty, including Deborah Sampson. However, women weren't allowed to be soldiers. To get around this, Sampson cut her hair and sewed men's clothes. In 1781 or 1782, she enlisted in the 4th Massachusetts Regiment of the Continental army—as a man. She used the fake name Robert Shurtliff.

Sampson fought in several tough battles and sometimes fought English soldiers hand-to-hand. She was injured many times, but often tended to her own wounds. She once tried to remove a musket ball from her thigh because she feared her fellow soldiers would discover she was a woman. After Sampson fell ill with a fever, a doctor finally learned her secret. She was given an **honorable discharge** in October 1783.

AMAZING ACHIEVEMENTS

In 1983, the state of Massachusetts named Sampson its official state heroine.

After leaving the army, Sampson had a hard time securing her pension, or payment in exchange for her service. Paul Revere wrote to Congress on her behalf, saying she was "more deserving than hundreds" of soldiers who had no problem receiving their pension.

LADY WITH THE LAMP

In 1854, the British government sent nurse Florence Nightingale on a mission to Turkey. English soldiers who had been wounded in the Crimean War were recovering there. The conditions of the military hospital were terrible. Nightingale found dirty, overcrowded rooms. There wasn't any soap or blankets, and soldiers' clothes were crawling with bugs. More soldiers were dying from infection and disease than from battle wounds.

Nightingale and her team worked hard to improve the hospital's conditions. They cleaned the wards and got soldiers food and other supplies they needed to get well. Nightingale was nicknamed the "lady with the lamp" because of her nights spent tending to bedridden patients. Nightingale learned much from her experience in a war hospital. When she returned to England, she helped reform the military medical system.

AMAZING ACHIEVEMENTS

Nightingale's 1859 book, *Notes on Nursing*, helped generations learn how to care for the sick and wounded. In 1860, she opened the Nightingale School of Nursing in London.

Nightingale is considered the founder of modern nursing. She made it a meaningful profession for women who wanted to work outside the home.

11

ANGEL OF THE BATTLEFIELD

When the Civil War began in 1861, a woman named Clara Barton was determined to help the hungry and wounded Union army soldiers she saw around her. Barton began collecting and handing out supplies to soldiers and later worked as a nurse. Though she wasn't actually in the military, she followed the troops to the battlefields of Antietam, Harpers Ferry, and Fredericksburg, risking her life to care for the soldiers. She became known as the "angel of the battlefield." After the war, Barton worked to reunite missing soldiers with their families.

In 1870, Barton was in Europe when the Franco-Prussian War broke out. She worked with a new aid organization called the Red Cross, which brought relief to people affected by the war. Barton was inspired to form a relief organization in the United States. The American Red Cross was officially founded in 1882.

AMAZING ACHIEVEMENTS

Barton led the American Red Cross for 23 years. Today, the organization provides aid to people affected by floods, hurricanes, fires, and war. Its mission also includes working with members of the military and helping them keep in touch with their families.

During the Civil War, Barton asked for donations, collected supplies, and bought them herself. She delivered the supplies to battlefields and helped organize and hand them out.

DOCTOR ON THE FRONT LINES

Dr. Mary Edwards Walker earned a medical degree in 1855 at a time when medicine was mostly limited to men. When the Civil War broke out, Walker cared for wounded soldiers in the Union army. She became the army's first female surgeon and worked in field hospitals on many battlefields.

In 1864, the Confederate army took Walker prisoner. After her release, she supervised a hospital for female prisoners and an orphanage. She received the Congressional Medal of Honor in 1865. She was the first woman to receive this award.

In 1917, Congress changed its standards for the Medal of Honor and withdrew Walker's honor. Walker refused to give back the medal and wore it every day until she died. In 1977, President Jimmy Carter restored Walker's Medal of Honor.

AMAZING ACHIEVEMENTS

The Congressional Medal of Honor is the United States' highest military award. Walker is the only woman who has ever received it.

Walker was a firm believer in women's rights. During her lifetime, women wore tight **corsets** and heavy skirts that limited their movement. Walker often wore men's clothing to protest what society expected of women.

BUFFALO SOLDIER

Cathay Williams was born into slavery around 1842 in Missouri. As a young girl, she was forced into work as a cook and washerwoman for the Union army during the Civil War, which brought her to battlefields in Arkansas, Louisiana, and Georgia. In 1866, a year after the war ended, Williams enlisted as a soldier in the army.

Disguised as a man and using the name William Cathay, Williams enlisted in the 38th U.S. Infantry. It was one of the all–African American U.S. Army regiments known as the Buffalo Soldiers. "Private Cathay" served for two years. She was the only woman known to have served as a Buffalo Soldier and the first documented African American woman to serve in the U.S. Army.

The famous abolitionist Harriet Tubman, pictured here, worked as a volunteer nurse, spy, and scout for the Union army during the Civil War.

RESISTANCE FIGHTER

Nancy Wake grew up in Australia and began her career as a journalist in Paris. When **Nazi** Germany invaded France in 1940 during World War II, she joined the French Resistance. This was a group that continued to fight Nazis after the French government surrendered. Wake delivered coded messages and supplies for **Allied** soldiers and helped people escape France. When the Nazis learned of her work and tried to arrest her, she escaped to England.

Wake then joined the British Special Operations Executive, which was a secret agency that specialized in undercover warfare. In April 1944, Wake parachuted into France. She collected weapons and equipment and hid them for Allied soldiers to find after they invaded France on **D-Day**. After D-Day, she fought in combat against Germans until the Nazis were defeated.

AMAZING ACHIEVEMENTS

Wake is credited with saving hundreds of lives thanks to her efforts in helping Jews and soldiers escape Nazi-occupied France.

Wake was the most decorated woman of World War II. Her honors include the George Medal from England, the Medal of Freedom from the U.S., and three Croix de Guerre from France.

FIRST IN FLIGHT

Olga Custodio had always dreamed of becoming a pilot. Born in Puerto Rico in 1954, she grew up traveling around the world as the daughter of an army officer. At 16, she tried to join the Reserve Officer Training Corps (ROTC), but was told women weren't allowed into the program. However, she didn't let that stop her from achieving her childhood dream.

When she was 25, Custodio finally joined the air force. She became the first Latina to complete U.S. Air Force military pilot training. She went on to teach other military pilots how to fly, breaking new ground for female flight instructors at Laughlin and Randolph Air Force Bases in Texas. She won an Aviation Safety Award for the way she handled an emergency after her plane hit some birds in bad weather.

AMAZING ACHIEVEMENTS

Custodio retired as a lieutenant colonel in 2003 after serving in the air force reserves for 24 years. She later became the first Latina commercial airline captain as a pilot for American Airlines.

Custodio has said her personal motto is "Querer es poder," meaning, if you want something to happen, you have to make it happen.

FOUR-STAR HEROES

Ann Dunwoody joined the army in 1975 and became a skilled parachutist. In 1992, she became the first woman battalion commander for the 82nd Airborne Division, which is a group that specializes in parachute assault operations. As her career developed, Dunwoody became an expert in **logistics**. Her job was to make sure troops in combat zones received all the ammunition, tanks, fuel, and other supplies they needed.

In 2008, Dunwoody made history when she became the first woman promoted to the position of four-star general, which is the highest rank in the armed services. She led the U.S. Army Materiel Command, where she was in charge of supplying equipment, arms, and uniforms to soldiers in Iraq and Afghanistan.

Two other women have earned a four-star rank since Dunwoody's groundbreaking achievement. In 2012, Janet Wolfenbarger became the air force's first female four-star general. In 2014, Michelle Howard became the first female and first African American woman to become a four-star admiral in the navy.

Ann Dunwoody

Janet Wolfenbarger

Michelle Howard

THE SURGEON GENERAL

Patricia Horoho has spent her career providing medical care in emergency situations. After receiving her nursing degree and training to treat **trauma**, Horoho joined the army and soon became head nurse of the emergency room at Womack Army Medical Center in Fort Bragg, North Carolina. During her service, she has provided critical aid at times of disaster, including giving first aid to 75 victims of the September 11 attacks on the **Pentagon** in 2001. She has also served in Afghanistan.

Horoho became head of the U.S. Army Nurse Corps in 2008. Three years later, President Barack Obama appointed her Surgeon General of the Army. She is the first nurse and the first woman to hold the position of the army's top medical officer.

AMAZING ACHIEVEMENTS

In 2002, the American Red Cross recognized Horoho as a Nurse Hero for her work after the September 11 attacks.

As Surgeon General of the Army, Patricia Horoho is in charge of America's third-largest health-care system, which cares for more than 3.5 million people around the world.

FIGHTING FOR VETERANS

Tammy Duckworth was working on her Ph.D. (the highest-level college degree) when she was **deployed** to Iraq as part of the Illinois Army National Guard. She was one of the first women to fly combat missions during Operation Iraqi Freedom.

In 2004, Duckworth was copiloting a helicopter when it was hit by a rocket-propelled grenade. She lost both her legs and partial use of her right arm. Duckworth was awarded the Air Medal, the Combat Action Badge, and the Purple Heart, but she wasn't done fighting.

As she recovered, Duckworth worked to provide **veterans** with better medical care. After she became assistant secretary for veteran affairs, she focused on helping homeless and female veterans. In 2012, Duckworth was elected to the U.S. House of Representatives, where she has continued to fight for veterans and their families.

Tammy Duckworth is the first disabled woman to serve in Congress. She is also the first Asian American congresswoman to represent Illinois.

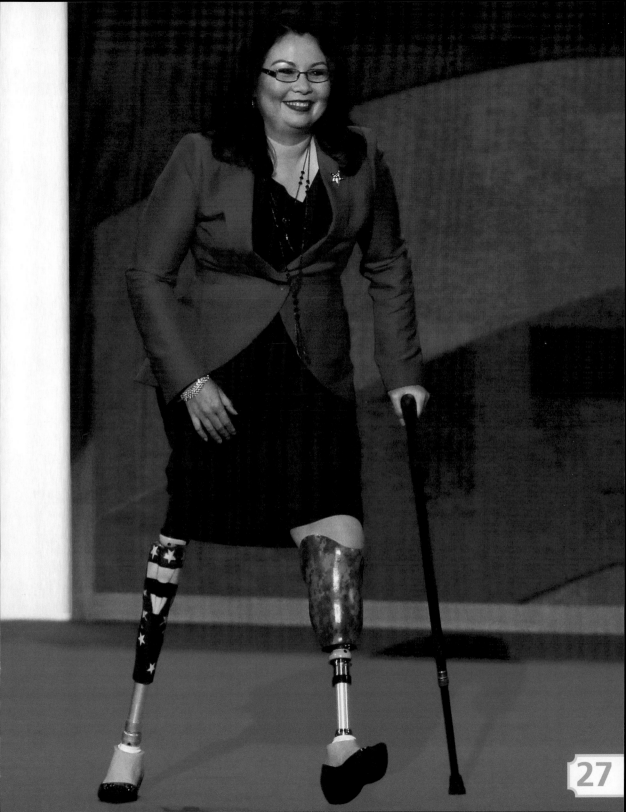

OPPORTUNITIES FOR WOMEN

More than 200,000 women serve in the U.S. military today. They currently make up almost 15 percent of American servicemembers. Like military women around the world, they risk their lives every day to protect their country. They can be found in every branch of the military, in every rank, and in nearly every position.

Although the roles available to women in the military have expanded a great deal over the past century, some barriers remain. In the U.S., women are kept from serving in combat positions. However, women have proven they have what it takes to fight. The movement to open all military positions to women keeps gaining ground, and the ban on women in combat may soon come to an end.

Many women in the armed forces have also achieved great things outside the military. Admiral Grace Hopper joined the U.S. Naval Reserves in 1943. She worked on a computer that made advanced calculations for the military. Later, she created the first program that turned human language into codes that machines could read.

TIMELINE OF WOMEN IN THE MILITARY

1429 - Joan of Arc leads French troops to victory against the English.

1781 or 1782 - During the American Revolution, Deborah Sampson enlists in the 4th Massachusetts Regiment under the name Robert Shurtliff.

1854 - Florence Nightingale treats British soldiers in Turkey during the Crimean War. Her experiences and knowledge lead to reform in military medicine.

1865 - Dr. Mary E. Walker becomes the first and only woman to receive the Congressional Medal of Honor for her service during the Civil War.

1866 - Cathay Williams enlists in the U.S. Army as William Cathay. She is the first documented African American woman to serve in the army.

1882 - Clara Barton helps to officially establish the American Red Cross.

1901 - The Army Nurse Corps is established. The Navy Nurse Corps is established seven years later.

1914–1918 - Around 33,000 women serve during World War I as nurses and support staff.

1939–1945 - More than 400,000 women serve in the U.S. military during World War II in noncombat jobs, including ambulance drivers, pilots, mechanics, and nurses. Women in Europe become resistance fighters and join civil defense units. In the Soviet Union, women perform combat roles in every branch of the armed forces.

1944 - Resistance fighter Nancy Wake parachutes into France before D-Day to gather and hide supplies for Allied soldiers.

1976 - The first women are admitted to the U.S. Military Academy at West Point, U.S. Naval Academy at Annapolis, and the U.S. Air Force Academy.

1979 - Olga Custodio is the first Latina to graduate from U.S. Air Force flight school.

1991 - Congress authorizes women to fly in combat missions. In 1993, Congress authorizes women to serve on combat ships.

2008 - Ann Dunwoody becomes the first woman promoted to the rank of four-star general.

2011 - Patricia Horoho becomes the first woman and first nurse appointed Surgeon General of the Army.

2012 - Veteran Tammy Duckworth becomes the first disabled woman elected to Congress.

GLOSSARY

Allied: Belonging to countries including the United States, United Kingdom, France, and Soviet Union that fought against the Axis powers during World War II.

battalion: A large body of troops ready for battle.

convoy: A group of ships or vehicles traveling together.

corset: A close-fitting undergarment worn by women.

D-Day: June 6, 1944. On this day, Allied forces landed in Normandy, France, to attack German forces. The successful attack led to an Allied victory in Europe.

deploy: To move troops into position for military action.

heresy: Beliefs that go against the teachings of a certain religion.

honorable discharge: Being let out of military service with a good record.

insurgent: A rebel.

logistics: The military science of moving, housing, and supplying troops and equipment.

Nazi: A member of the National Socialist German Workers' Party, which led Germany from 1933 until 1945, when World War II ended.

Pentagon: The headquarters of the United States Department of Defense.

trauma: Extreme physical or emotional injury.

valor: Great courage in the face of danger.

veteran: A person who has served in the military.

INDEX

WEBSITES

Due to the changing nature of Internet links, PowerKids Press has developed an online list of websites related to the subject of this book. This site is updated regularly. Please use this link to access the list: www.powerkidslinks.com/wmng/mili